HINA

and the

Sea of Stars

$10.95

Adapted and Illustrated by

Michael Nordenstrom

3565 Harding Ave.
Honolulu, Hawai'i 96816
Phone: (808) 734-7159
Toll Free: (800) 910-2377
Fax: (808) 732-3627
www.besspress.com

BESS PRESS

Design: Carol Colbath

Library of Congress Cataloging-in-Publication Data

Nordenstrom, Michael.
Hina and the sea of stars / adapted
and illustrated by Michael Nordenstrom ;
p. cm.
Includes illustrations, glossary.
ISBN 1-57306-167-0
1. Hina (Hawaiian deity) - Juvenile
literature. 2. Goddesses - Hawaii -
Juvenile literature 3. Mythology,
Hawaiian - Juvenile literature.
4. Folklore - Hawaii - Juvenile
literature. I. Title.
GR510.N68 2003   299.92-dc21

Printed in China

03 04 05 06 07 08   6 5 4 3 2 1

In respect for Hina,
and for Maria,
the Goddess of Breakfast

On nights when the moon is full, you can see Hina,
the mother of the Hawaiian people, making *kapa*.
It is because of Hina that the moon and stars
shine over the sleeping world below. And it is Hina's *kapa*
that encircles the earth and forms clouds.

4

Hina has not always lived on the moon.
She began her life in Kahikihonuakele,
under the sea, where she lived with
her fish parents and many brothers
and sisters.

Her favorite brother was Kīpapa.
He promised their parents
that he would protect Hina,
but he was usually off swimming
with his ocean friends.

8

This made his parents angry, and one day
they banished him to the deepest part of the sea.
Would he ever see his sister again?

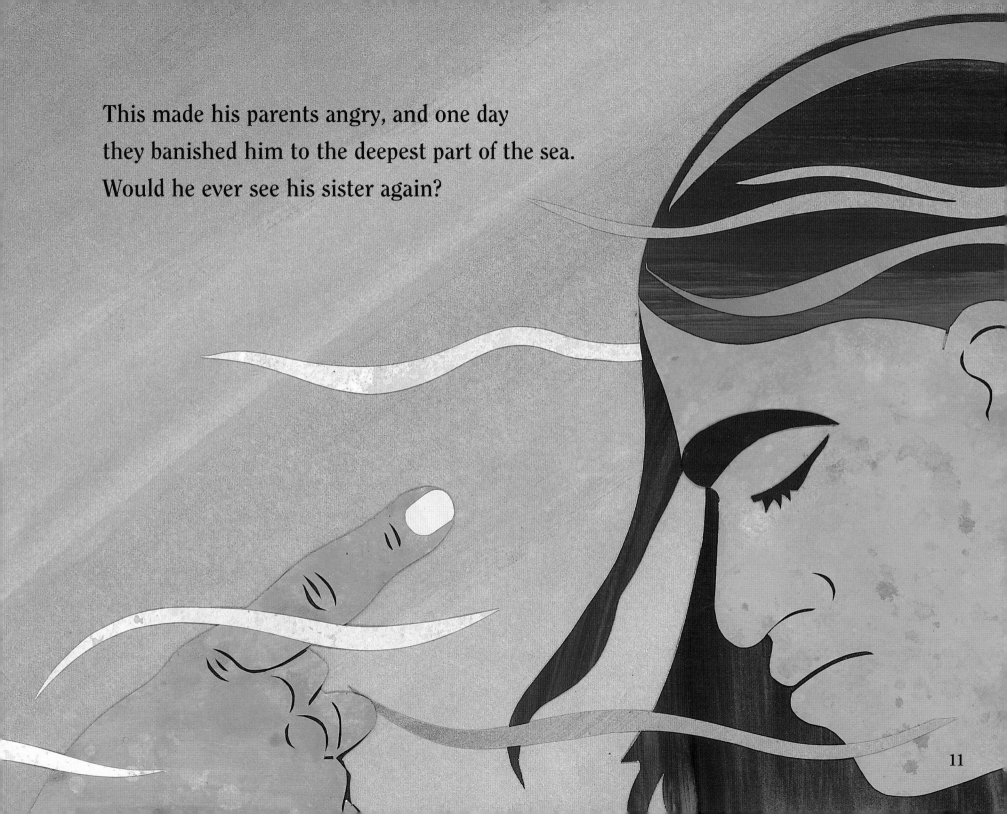

Wanting to leave something behind for Hina,
Kīpapa quickly filled a calabash
with starfish and a crescent moon.
This gift would remind Hina of his love.

13

Then,
sad and alone,
he journeyed to the deepest part of the sea.
His grandfather could not bear to see him
in such misery, so he stirred up a mighty tempest.
Dark waves surged, and with a mighty thunder the sea floor

CRACKED!

Kīpapa crawled through the opening until he reached the Hawaiian Islands.

Kīpapa was befriended by Chief Konikonia, who taught him the ways of the Islanders. Konikonia asked Kīpapa to return to the sea and bring Hina back to live with them.

Hina and Kīpapa had a joyful reunion,
and Hina agreed to return with him.
She took the calabash with her
to remind her of the sea.

However, when Hina left the sea, the stars and moon f l o a t e d up into the evening sky. The stars drifted away until they were only faint points of light. The moon stayed close and grew larger, bathing the world with its light.

When Chief Konikonia and Hina met,
they fell in love.
Together they had ten children.
When these children grew,
they had their own families, and eventually
there were as many people on the islands
as there were stars in the heavens.

24

With her children grown,
Hina now longed to leave the earth
and find a place where she could be alone.
She made a colorful *kapa* and threw it high into the air.
That *kapa* became the first rainbow.

Hina climbed the rainbow until she reached the sun.
But when she got there, she found it was

too hot!

So when night came,
she lowered herself
onto the moon.

It was just right.

And there she has
remained ever since,
making *kapa*
and watching over her
children from above.

29

Now, at night, the whales in Waimea Bay
wave at their friend in the moon
and know that it will be another good night.

Glossary

Hina (HEE nah): a Polynesian goddess considered to be a primary ancestor of the Hawaiian people. In Hawaiian mythology, Hina is often associated with the moon and its cycles, and therefore with fishing, planting, and fertility.

kapa (KAH pah): cloth made from bark.

Kahikihonuakele (kah HEE kee hoh noo ah KEH leh): a land under the sea.

Kīpapa (KEE pah pah): Hina's younger brother.

calabash: a container made from a hollowed-out gourd.

Konikonia (koh nee koh NEE ah): a chief of Hilo, Hawai'i.

Waimea (wye MAY ah) **Bay**: a bay on the North Shore of O'ahu; also, the bay in southwest Kaua'i where Captain Cook first landed.

Sources

Hina and the Sea of Stars combines elements of several legends about Hina described in Martha Beckwith's *Hawaiian Mythology* (Honolulu: University of Hawai'i Press, 1970).

Michael Nordenstrom is Associate Librarian and Volunteer Coordinator at the Salt Lake City Public Library. His love for art and anthropology and his belief in preserving legends inspired *Hina and the Sea of Stars* and his previous book, *Pele and the Rivers of Fire*, which won a Hawai'i Publishers Association Pa'i award for illustration and was a finalist for the Utah Children's Book Award. In depicting the goddess Hina's movement from sea to land to sky, Michael uses paint and collage to create rich, colorful, three-dimensional shapes and clear images. Visit his Web site to learn more: www.RiversofFire.com